C000256832

WARSAW

A POCKET TRAVEL GUIDE

2024

Your Updated and Comprehensive travel Companion for exploring the top attractions and off the beaten path of Poland capital city

JAMES D. FLICK

WARSAW MAP

TABLE OF CONTENT

WELCOME TO WARSAW

Warsaw, the energetic capital of Poland, is located in the center of the country, where modernism and tradition coexist. Greetings from a city that has risen beyond its turbulent past to become a symbol of resiliency and cultural vibrancy. Warsaw has a tapestry of experiences just waiting to be found, from its cobblestone streets decorated with the remnants of bygone centuries to the shining skyscrapers that embody its forward-looking mentality.

Get ready to explore a city that has witnessed a long history of victories and setbacks. Enjoy the contrast between modern art installations and Warsaw's historical architectural treasures, which each tell a different tale of the city's development.

We cordially welcome you to explore the Old Town's maze-like lanes with this guide, where the painstakingly restored façade reverberates with historical echoes. Explore the splendor of royal palaces, lush gardens, and museums that honor the city's unwavering character as you travel through time. Savor the fragrant joys of traditional Polish cuisine and immerse yourself in the vibrant cultural scene that permeates the city's streets.

Come along on an exploration of Warsaw's past, present, and future as we unearth the mysteries concealed in its districts and reveal the beauty and attraction that set this place apart. So come on this journey with us and let Warsaw capture your thoughts, making a lasting impression on your travel diaries. Welcome to Warsaw, a city whose fascinating fabric tells a tale around every corner.

Tips for Traveling in Warsaw

With the help of these invaluable travel advice, get ready to make the most of your trip to Warsaw:

- **Public Transportation Mastery**: Make use of Warsaw's well-functioning bus and tram systems. If you want to save money at attractions and enjoy unrestricted travel, think about getting a Warsaw Tourist Card.
- Accept the Variations of Warsaw's Seasons with Seasonal Sensibility. Winter provides a wonderful atmosphere with its snowy landscapes and holiday markets, while summer brings colorful festivals and outdoor festivities.

- Cultural Curiosity: Pick up a few simple Polish phrases to start a conversation with locals. Often, the effort pays off with kind interactions and unforgettable moments.
- Exploration Strategy: To get a closer look at Old Town's ancient charm, take a stroll along its cobblestone lanes in the calmer early morning or evening hours.
- Museum Navigation: To save as much money as possible, schedule your trips during the hours or days when many museums provide free entrance.
- Gastronomic Adventures: Taste authentic Polish cuisine from neighborhood restaurants and street vendors, such as pierogi (dumplings), żurek (sour rye soup), and oscypek (smoked cheese).
- Weather rediness: The weather in Warsaw is erratic. Carry an umbrella and wear layers of clothing to be ready for unexpected downpours or temperature swings.
- Cash vs. Card: Although most places take cards, it's a good idea to have some Polish złoty on hand for smaller vendors or neighborhood markets.
- Exploration with Dignity: Keep in mind to observe any clothing restrictions or guidelines and show respect when you visit religious monuments or memorials.
- Local Insider Knowledge: Seize the opportunity to converse with locals; their knowledge frequently leads to unexpected discoveries and a more profound comprehension of Warsaw's culture.

These recommendations are designed to improve your trip, so you can easily explore Warsaw and fully immerse yourself in its rich cultural heritage. As you tour this fascinating city, get ready to make memories that will last a lifetime.

CHAPTER 1: GETTING ACQUAINTED WITH WARSAW

1.1 Overview of Warsaw"

Delve into the heartbeat of Poland with an immersive overview of Warsaw, a city steeped in history, adorned with resilience, and pulsating with contemporary energy.

A Tapestry of History and Modernity

As the capital city, Warsaw embodies the spirit of a nation that has traversed tumultuous epochs. Once ravaged by wars and conflicts, it has emerged as a testament to resilience, showcasing a fusion of architectural marvels that narrate tales of triumph and revival.

A Glimpse into Warsaw's Past

Tracing its roots back to the 13th century, Warsaw's narrative encompasses royal legacies, tumultuous uprisings, and the struggles of a city reborn. Witness the echoes of its storied past through the meticulously reconstructed Old Town, designated a UNESCO World Heritage Site, where each cobblestone whispers tales of resilience and restoration.

Warsaw Today:

Amidst its historic grandeur, Warsaw thrives as a dynamic metropolis, adorned with sleek skyscrapers and a buzzing cosmopolitan vibe. Explore the bustling streets teeming with cultural hotspots, lively markets, and a vibrant arts scene, showcasing a city that harmonizes its rich heritage with contemporary allure.

An Overview to Guide Your Exploration

This section serves as your compass, providing a panoramic glimpse into Warsaw's soul. From its historical significance to its current urban fabric, it lays the foundation for an enriching journey through the myriad facets of this multifaceted city. Prepare to embark on a captivating expedition through Warsaw's intriguing landscapes and diverse tapestry, embracing its past while reveling in its present vitality.

1.2 Brief History of Warsaw

Discover the fascinating tale of Warsaw, a city that has persevered through hardships and victories as seen through its rich past.

The Establishment of a Capital

The history of Warsaw begins in the thirteenth century, when it was just a little village on the banks of the Vistula River. It developed into a major strategic center over time, and in the late 16th century, under King Sigismund III Vasa's reign, it was named the capital of Poland.

Uncertain Times and Fortitude

With a history dotted with invasions, uprisings, and wars, Warsaw's fortitude was put to the test time and time again. The city saw the destruction caused by war, most notably World War II, which left almost 85% of its architectural legacy in ruins. Nevertheless, it rose from the ashes with a resolve to restore and revitalize its core.

The Warsaw Uprising and Reconstruction Following the War

The heroic Warsaw Uprising of 1944 is remembered as a pivotal moment in the history of the city and as a symbol of defiance against oppression. Massive post-war reconstruction efforts resulted in the thorough restoration of the city's important landmarks, including the Old Town, giving its historic center new life.

From the Soviet Era to the Current Renaissance

The Soviet era brought hardships to Warsaw, including political upheavals and sociocultural shifts. But when Poland became a democratic nation in 1989, Warsaw welcomed a new period of development and modernization. It is now a thriving capital city in Europe that successfully blends its rich history with a modern perspective.

A Tapestry Crafted with Tradition and Modification

Warsaw's history is a moving story of resiliency, tenacity, and adaptation. Warsaw's identity is a reflection of its journey through the ages, from the echoes of its royal past to the throbbing rhythms of its modern cosmopolitan spirit.

Get ready to dive into the many facets of Warsaw's past and discover the essence of the city by looking through its fascinating glass.

1.3 Seasons and Best Times to Visit

When planning your trip to Warsaw, it's essential to consider the city's distinct seasons and determine the best time to visit based on your preferences and desired activities. Warsaw's climate is characterized by warm summers, cool winters, and pleasant spring and autumn seasons.

Seasons

Warsaw has four distinct seasons:

- Spring (March-May): Spring in Warsaw is a delightful time of year, with temperatures gradually warming up and the city bursting into bloom. The average temperature in Warsaw in spring ranges from 4°C to 19°C (39°F to 66°F).

- Summer (June-August): Summer is the most popular time to visit Warsaw, as the weather is warm and sunny. The average temperature in Warsaw in summer ranges from 17°C to 25°C (63°F to 77°F).

- Autumn (September-November): Autumn is a beautiful time to visit Warsaw, as the leaves change color and the city takes on a cozy atmosphere. The average temperature in Warsaw in autumn ranges from 7°C to 16°C (45°F to 61°F).

- Winter (December-February): Winter in Warsaw is cold and snowy, but the city is still charming and festive during the holiday season. The average temperature in Warsaw in winter ranges from -2°C to 5°C (29°F to 41°F).

Best Times to Visit

The best time to visit Warsaw depends on your personal preferences and what you want to experience. Here are some suggestions:

- For warm weather and outdoor activities: The best time to visit Warsaw for warm weather and outdoor activities is during the summer months (June-August). However, keep in mind that summer is also the peak tourist season, so prices will be higher and crowds will be larger.

- For fewer crowds and lower prices: If you prefer fewer crowds and lower prices, consider visiting Warsaw during the shoulder seasons (spring or autumn). The weather is still pleasant during these months, and you'll have more opportunities to enjoy the city's attractions without the summer rush.

- For a festive atmosphere: The best time to visit Warsaw for a festive atmosphere is during the holiday season (December-January). The city is decorated with lights and festive decorations, and there are many Christmas markets and events to enjoy.

Ultimately, the best time to visit Warsaw is whenever you have the opportunity to travel and enjoy the city's unique charm and attractions.

CHAPTER 2: NAVIGATING WARSAW

2.1 Transportation Options

Warsaw, Poland's vibrant capital, offers a diverse range of transportation options to suit every traveler's needs and preferences. Whether you're seeking a quick and efficient commute, a leisurely exploration of the city's landmarks, or an eco-friendly way to get around, Warsaw has you covered.

Public Transportation

Warsaw's public transportation system is extensive, reliable, and affordable, making it an excellent choice for getting around the city. The system consists of:

- Metro: Warsaw's metro system is the backbone of public transportation, with two lines (M1 and M2) that connect various districts and major attractions. The metro operates from 5:00 AM to 1:00 AM.

- Buses: Warsaw has an extensive bus network that covers the entire city and beyond. Buses operate from 5:00 AM to midnight, with some routes running 24 hours a day.

- Trams: Trams are a popular and convenient way to travel around Warsaw, particularly in the city center. Trams operate from 5:00 AM to 11:00 PM.

- Night Buses: For late-night travel, Warsaw offers a network of night buses that operate from midnight to 5:00 AM.

Tickets for public transportation can be purchased from ticket machines at metro stations, bus stops, and kiosks. Single-journey tickets, valid for one ride on any public transportation mode, are available. For more frequent travelers, 24-hour, 72-hour, and monthly passes are also offered.

Taxis and Ride-Hailing Services

Taxis and ride-hailing services like Uber and Bolt are readily available in Warsaw and provide a convenient and comfortable way to get around. Taxis can be requested via a taxi app or hailed on the street. Ride-hailing services can be booked using their respective apps.

Cycling and Walking

Warsaw is a relatively pedestrian-friendly city, with many dedicated bike lanes and pedestrian zones. Bicycling is a common way of transportation for both locals and tourists. Warsaw also offers a network of shared bicycles, which can be rented and parked at designated stations.

Private Transportation

If you prefer the convenience of private transportation, car rental services are available at Warsaw Chopin Airport and various locations in the city. However, it's important to note that parking in Warsaw can be challenging and expensive, especially in the city center.

Airport Transportation

Warsaw Chopin Airport (WAW) is well-connected to the city center by various transportation options:

- Kolej Mazowiecka Train: The KM train connects the airport to the city center in about 20 minutes.

- City Bus: City buses 175 and 188 connect the airport to the city center.

- Taxis and Ride-Hailing Services: Taxis and ride-hailing services are readily available at the airport.

Additional Tips

- Plan your route in advance: Use a map app or public transportation website to plan your route and check for any disruptions or delays.

- Purchase tickets in advance: If you plan to use public transportation frequently, consider purchasing a multi-day pass to save money.

- Validate your ticket: Once you board a public transportation vehicle, validate your ticket at the designated machine to avoid fines.

- Be aware of your surroundings: Keep an eye on your belongings and be aware of your surroundings, especially in crowded areas.

- Learn basic Polish phrases: Learning a few basic Polish phrases will enhance your interactions with locals and make your trip more enjoyable.

Warsaw's diverse range of transportation options ensures that you can easily navigate the city and explore its many attractions. Whether you choose to rely on public transportation, taxis, ride-hailing services, cycling, or walking, you'll find a convenient and efficient way to get around and experience the vibrant capital of Poland.

2.2 Where to Stay

Warsaw offers a wide variety of accommodation options to suit all budgets, from luxury hotels to budget hostels. Here are a few of the best places to stay in Warsaw:

- **Luxury:**

    - Hotel Bristol: A 5-star hotel located in the heart of Warsaw, the Hotel Bristol is a luxurious and elegant choice. The hotel offers a variety of amenities, including a spa, fitness center, and several restaurants.
    - Raffles Europejski Warsaw: Another 5-star hotel, the Raffles Europejski Warsaw is located in a historic building that was once a palace. The hotel offers a variety of amenities, including a spa, fitness center, and several restaurants.

- **Mid-range:**

    - InterContinental Warsaw: A 4-star hotel located in the city center, the InterContinental Warsaw is a modern and stylish choice. The hotel offers a variety of amenities, including a spa, fitness center, and several restaurants.

    - Hotel MDM: A 4-star hotel located in the city center, the Hotel MDM is a historic and elegant choice. The hotel offers a variety of amenities, including a spa, fitness center, and several restaurants.

- **Budget:**
  - Hostel Warsaw: A centrally located hostel, Hostel Warsaw offers clean and comfortable accommodation at a reasonable price. The hostel has a variety of amenities, including a common room, kitchen, and laundry facilities.
  - Chillout Hostel: Another centrally located hostel, Chillout Hostel offers clean and comfortable accommodation at a reasonable price. The hostel has a variety of amenities, including a common room, kitchen, and laundry facilities.

When choosing where to stay in Warsaw, consider your budget, your desired location, and the amenities that are important to you.

Here are some additional tips for finding a place to stay in Warsaw:

- Book your accommodation in advance: Warsaw is a popular tourist destination, so it is advisable to book your accommodation in advance, especially if you are visiting during the peak season.

- Consider your location: Warsaw is a large city, so it is important to consider your location when choosing a place to stay. If you want to be in the heart of the action, choose a hotel in the city center. If you are on a budget, consider staying in a hostel in a more affordable neighborhood.

- Read reviews: Before booking your accommodation, be sure to read reviews from other guests. This can help you get a sense of the hotel or hostel and make sure it is a good fit for you.

2.3 Dining and Cuisine

Warsaw offers a vibrant and diverse culinary scene, reflecting its rich history and cultural influences. From traditional Polish fare to international cuisine, the city's restaurants and cafes cater to a wide range of tastes and budgets. Whether you're seeking hearty dumplings, authentic borscht, or a taste of global flavors, Warsaw's dining scene will not disappoint.

Polish Culinary Delights

Embark on a culinary adventure through Poland's culinary heritage by savoring these iconic dishes:

- Pierogi: These delectable dumplings, filled with savory or sweet fillings like potatoes, cheese, meat, or fruit, are a staple of Polish cuisine.

- Borscht: This hearty soup, typically made with beetroot, vegetables, and meat, is a comforting and nourishing dish.

- Żurek: This sour rye soup, often served with boiled egg and white sausage, is a traditional Polish delicacy.

- Bigos: This rich and flavorful stew, featuring a blend of sauerkraut, meat, and various vegetables, is a Polish culinary gem.

- Kotlet Schabowy: This breaded pork cutlet, a beloved Polish comfort food, is often served with potatoes and a simple salad.

International Culinary Delights

Venture beyond traditional Polish cuisine and explore the city's international culinary scene:

- Italian Cuisine: Indulge in authentic Italian flavors, from wood-fired pizzas and pasta dishes to creamy risottos and delicate tiramisu.

- Asian Cuisine: Experience the diverse flavors of Asia, from fragrant Thai curries and spicy Sichuan dishes to delicate sushi and savory Vietnamese pho.

- Middle Eastern Cuisine: Savor the aromatic spices and textures of Middle Eastern cuisine, from hummus and falafel to grilled meats and baklava.

- Latin American Cuisine: Immerse yourself in the vibrant flavors of Latin America, from fiery Mexican tacos and cheesy Brazilian churrasco to hearty Peruvian ceviche and tangy Argentinian empanadas.

Dining Recommendations

Its path of my duty to provide a guide for your culinary exploration of Warsaw, here are some highly-rated restaurants representing various cuisines:

- **Polish Cuisine:**

  - Giermek: This traditional Polish restaurant offers a charming ambiance and authentic dishes like pierogi, żurek, and bigos.

  - Zapiecek: This casual eatery serves up generous portions of Polish home-style cooking, including hearty soups, stews, and dumplings.

- **International Cuisine:**

  - La Cucina dei Quattro Mori: This elegant Italian restaurant showcases authentic flavors with its wood-fired pizzas, pasta dishes, and delectable desserts.

- Chimera: This vibrant Asian fusion restaurant offers a creative blend of Thai, Vietnamese, and Chinese cuisine, catering to diverse palates.

- Beirut Lebanese Restaurant: This cozy eatery transports you to Lebanon with its aromatic mezze platters, grilled meats, and traditional sweets.

- La Vera Enchilada: This lively Mexican restaurant brings the flavors of Mexico to Warsaw, offering tacos, burritos, enchiladas, and margaritas.

Dining Tips

To enhance your dining experience in Warsaw, consider these helpful tips:

- Reservations: For popular restaurants, especially during peak hours, it is advisable to make reservations in advance.

- Tipping: Tipping is customary in Warsaw, with a standard tip of 10-15% of the bill.

- English Menu Availability: Check if the restaurant provides English menus, or be prepared with a translation app if necessary.

- Local Specialties: Embrace the opportunity to try local specialties and traditional dishes to experience Poland's culinary heritage.

- Neighborhood Exploration: Venture beyond the city center to discover hidden culinary gems in different neighborhoods.

With its diverse and vibrant culinary scene, Warsaw offers a delightful dining experience for every taste and budget. Embark on a culinary adventure, savor the authentic flavors of Poland, and explore the global tastes that enrich the city's dining landscape.

2.4 Currency and Money Matters

Navigating the financial aspects of your trip to Warsaw is essential for a smooth and enjoyable experience. Understanding the local currency, exchange rates, and payment options will ensure you can manage your finances effectively throughout your stay.

Official Currency:

The official currency of Poland is the Polish złoty (PLN). Coins come in denominations of 1, 2, 5, 10, 20, and 50 groszy, while banknotes come in denominations of 10, 20, 50, 100, 200, and 500 PLN.

Currency Exchange:

Currency exchange services are readily available in Warsaw, including banks, exchange bureaus, and some hotels. Exchange rates vary depending on the institution and market conditions, so it's advisable to compare rates before exchanging currency. ATMs are also widely available and offer a convenient way to withdraw Polish złoty using your international debit or credit card.

Payment Methods:

Warsaw offers a mix of cash and contactless payment options. While cash is still widely accepted, contactless payments using credit cards, debit cards, or mobile payment apps are increasingly prevalent. Many stores, restaurants, and transportation services accept contactless payments, providing a convenient and secure way to make transactions.

Tips for Managing Finances:

- Inform Your Bank: Notify your bank about your travel plans to avoid any issues with using your cards abroad.

- Carry a Mix of Payment Options: Have a combination of cash and credit or debit cards to accommodate different payment situations.

- Be Mindful of Fees: Check with your bank for any international transaction fees or ATM withdrawal fees that may apply.

- Compare Exchange Rates: Shop around for the best exchange rates when converting currencies.

- Use Contactless Payments: Whenever possible, utilize contactless payment methods for their convenience and security.

By understanding the local currency, exchange rates, and payment options, you can confidently manage your finances during your trip to Warsaw and focus on enjoying the city's many attractions and experiences.

CHAPTER 3: EXPLORING WARSAW'S LANDMARKS

3.1 Old Town

Step into the heart of Warsaw, where history whispers from ancient cobblestone streets and captivating architecture unfolds around every corner. Welcome to Warsaw's Old Town, a UNESCO World Heritage Site that beckons with its rich tapestry of culture, history, and captivating charm.

A Stroll Through Time

Begin your exploration at the Royal Castle, a majestic symbol of Poland's regal past. Admire its grandeur, stroll through its courtyards, and immerse yourself in the stories of Polish monarchs who once resided within its walls.

Next, wander through the vibrant Old Town Market Square, the bustling hub of Old Town. Soak in the lively atmosphere, admire the colorful facades of surrounding buildings, and perhaps indulge in a traditional Polish delicacy at one of the many cafes or restaurants.

Delve into the spiritual realm at St. John's Cathedral, a masterpiece of Gothic architecture that has stood sentinel over Warsaw for centuries. Gaze upon its awe-inspiring spires and intricate stained-glass windows, and feel the tranquility that permeates its hallowed halls.

Unveiling Hidden Gems

Venture beyond the main attractions and discover the hidden gems that add to Old Town's allure. Seek out the Barbican, a remnant of Warsaw's medieval fortifications, and imagine the city's storied past.

Explore the University of Warsaw, a prestigious institution that has nurtured generations of scholars and intellectuals. Stroll through its picturesque courtyards and admire its neoclassical architecture.

Immerse yourself in art at the National Gallery of Art, home to an impressive collection of Polish and European paintings. Discover masterpieces by renowned artists and gain a deeper appreciation for Poland's rich artistic heritage.

3.2 Royal Castle and Castle Square

In the heart of Warsaw, Poland, stands an icon of the city's rich history – the Royal Castle. This majestic edifice, once the residence of Polish monarchs, now serves as a museum, its walls whispering tales of centuries past.

A Walk-Through History

Your Warsaw adventure continues in Castle Square, a vibrant plaza teeming with life. As you approach the Royal Castle, its imposing stature commands attention. The castle's Baroque architecture, a blend of grandeur and elegance, reflects the opulence of the Polish monarchy.

Step through the grand entrance and embark on a journey through time. The castle's interior is a treasure trove of art and artifacts, each piece narrating a chapter in Poland's history.

Admire the Royal Apartments, where monarchs once resided, and marvel at the exquisite collection of paintings, sculptures, and furniture.

A Glimpse into Royal Life

Wander through the Throne Room, where kings and queens held court, and imagine the grandeur of royal ceremonies. Ascend the Grand Staircase, its sweeping curves once graced by the footsteps of royalty.

Explore the Ballroom, where the aristocracy danced the night away, and envision the elegance of bygone eras. The castle's chapel, a sanctuary of serenity, offers a moment of quiet contemplation.

Emerging from the Castle

After immersing yourself in the castle's rich history, step back into Castle Square, where the city's vibrant energy awaits. Stroll along the cobblestone streets, lined with charming cafes and shops, and soak in the lively atmosphere.

Venture beyond the square and explore the surrounding streets, where historic buildings and modern attractions intertwine. Discover Sigismund's Column, a towering monument commemorating the victory over the Teutonic Knights, and admire the grandeur of the Presidential Palace.

A visit to the Royal Castle and Castle Square is a journey into Poland's royal past, a chance to connect with the country's rich history and admire the enduring beauty of its architectural heritage. From its majestic interiors to its lively surroundings, the Royal Castle and Castle Square offer a captivating glimpse into the heart of Warsaw.

3.3 Łazienki Park and Palace on the Water

Nestled amidst the bustling city of Warsaw lies an oasis of tranquility — Łazienki Park, a sprawling expanse of greenery adorned with picturesque landscapes, serene lakes, and architectural gems. Among its many treasures, the Palace on the Water stands as a captivating symbol of elegance and artistry.

A Stroll Through Nature's Embrace

Enter Łazienki Park through its grand gates and let the cares of the city melt away as you immerse yourself in the park's serene embrace. Winding pathways lead through verdant forests, past tranquil lakes, and across lush meadows, offering a delightful escape from the urban landscape.

As you wander along, admire the meticulously manicured gardens, where vibrant blooms and sculpted hedges create a masterpiece of horticultural artistry. Pause by the serene lakes, where swans glide gracefully across the water's surface, and let the gentle sounds of nature soothe your soul.

A Palace Fit for a King

Venture towards the heart of the park, where the Palace on the Water emerges from the lake's embrace. This exquisite structure, once the summer residence of Polish kings, is a masterpiece of Baroque architecture.

Step onto the palace's grand terrace and marvel at its reflection mirrored on the lake's surface. The palace's exterior, adorned with intricate carvings and statues, exudes an air of regal elegance.

Exploring the Palace's Treasures

Embark on a journey through the palace's opulent interior, where time seems to stand still. Admire the richly decorated chambers, adorned with fine art, exquisite furnishings, and intricate tapestries.

Ascend the grand staircase, its sweeping curves once graced by the footsteps of royalty, and explore the palace's many galleries and exhibitions. Discover the fascinating stories of the Polish monarchs who once called this palace home.

A Moment of Serenity

Seek refuge in the palace's enchanting Orangery, a glass-enclosed haven filled with exotic plants and flowers. The Orangery's tranquil atmosphere offers a moment of serenity, a perfect escape from the palace's grandeur.

3.4 Warsaw Uprising Museum

In the heart of Warsaw, Poland, stands a poignant reminder of the city's tumultuous past – the Warsaw Uprising Museum. This evocative institution chronicles the 63-day uprising of 1944, when the Polish resistance fought against Nazi occupation.

A Journey Through Time

Step through the museum's entrance and embark on a journey through time, a journey that will transport you to the heart of the Warsaw Uprising. Interactive exhibits, multimedia presentations, and personal artifacts bring the events of 1944 to life.

Wander through recreated scenes of everyday life during the uprising, from underground bunkers to makeshift hospitals. Witness the resilience of ordinary people who transformed into fearless fighters, risking their lives for freedom.

Stories of Courage and Sacrifice

Delve into the stories of individuals who played a pivotal role in the uprising, from young volunteers to experienced soldiers. Admire their courage, their determination, and their unwavering belief in a free Poland.

As you explore the museum's exhibits, you'll encounter poignant reminders of the uprising's toll – the destruction of the city, the loss of innocent lives, and the enduring scars of war.

A Testament to the Human Spirit

Despite the hardships and sacrifices, the Warsaw Uprising Museum serves as a testament to the resilience of the human spirit. It is a story of courage, determination, and the unwavering belief in freedom.

As you leave the museum, carry with you the echoes of history and the enduring legacy of the Warsaw Uprising. The museum's poignant exhibits and powerful stories will forever be etched in your memory, a reminder of the indomitable human spirit.

3.5 Wilanów Palace and Gardens

Just a short drive from Warsaw, Poland, lies a hidden gem – Wilanów Palace and Gardens. This UNESCO World Heritage Site is a stunning example of Baroque architecture and landscape design, and was once the summer residence of King Jan III Sobieski.

A Royal Retreat

Wilanów Palace was built in the early 17th century by King Jan III Sobieski, a Polish king and military leader who is considered one of the greatest Polish monarchs. The palace was designed to be a luxurious retreat for the king and his family, and it quickly became a center of Polish culture and politics.

The Palace's Exterior

The exterior of the palace is a magnificent example of Baroque design. The façade is adorned with intricate carvings and statues, and the roof is crowned with a golden dome. The palace's interior is equally impressive, with lavishly decorated chambers and galleries.

The Gardens

The palace is surrounded by beautiful gardens, which are divided into two sections: the upper garden and the lower garden. The upper garden is a formal garden with geometric patterns of flowers, trees, and fountains. The lower garden is a more natural garden with winding paths, ponds, and statues.

A Day at Wilanów Palace

A visit to Wilanów Palace and Gardens is a must for any visitor to Warsaw. The palace is a fascinating glimpse into Polish history and culture, and the gardens are a peaceful oasis in the heart of the city.

Here is a suggested itinerary for a day trip to Wilanów Palace and Gardens:

- Morning: Arrive at Wilanów Palace and Gardens and purchase your tickets. Start your visit with a tour of the palace, which will take you through the king's and queen's apartments, the State Rooms, and the Picture Gallery.

- Afternoon: After your tour, explore the gardens. Take a walk through the upper garden, admiring the formal gardens and fountains. Then, head to the lower garden for a more relaxed stroll.

- Evening: Have dinner at one of the many restaurants in the area.

Here are some additional tips for visiting Wilanów Palace and Gardens:

- The palace and gardens are open year-round. The best time to visit is during the spring or summer, when the weather is warm and sunny.

- The palace is wheelchair accessible.

- There is a free shuttle bus that runs from the Wilanów metro station to the palace.

I hope you enjoy you will enjoybyour visit to Wilanów Palace and Gardens!

CHAPTER 4: IMMERSING IN WARSAW'S CULTURE

Warsaw offers a vibrant and diverse cultural scene, with a wide range of festivals and events throughout the year. From traditional Polish celebrations to international arts and music festivals, there's something for everyone to enjoy.

4.1 Local Festivals and Events

Warsaw's cultural calendar is packed with exciting events that showcase the city's rich heritage and vibrant spirit. Here are some of the most popular local festivals and events:

- Warsaw Chopin Festival: This prestigious music festival, held every five years, celebrates the life and works of Frédéric Chopin, Poland's renowned composer. The festival features a series of concerts, recitals, and masterclasses by world-renowned pianists.

- Warsaw Contemporary Music Festival: This annual festival explores the latest trends in contemporary music, featuring performances by international and Polish composers and musicians. The festival also includes workshops, seminars, and exhibitions.

- Warsaw Jewish Culture Festival: This vibrant festival celebrates the rich cultural heritage of Warsaw's Jewish community. The festival features concerts, theater performances, film screenings, and exhibitions that explore Jewish history, tradition, and art.

- Warsaw Dance Festival: This international dance festival showcases a diverse range of dance styles, from classical ballet to contemporary dance. The festival features performances by international and Polish dance companies, as well as workshops and seminars.

- Warsaw Film Festival: This annual film festival presents a selection of international and Polish films, with a focus on independent and experimental cinema. The festival also includes workshops, seminars, and discussions with filmmakers.

- Warsaw Fringe Festival: This alternative theater festival presents a diverse range of theater productions, from traditional plays to experimental performances. The festival features performances by Polish and international theater companies, as well as workshops and seminars.

- Orange Warsaw Festival: This popular music festival features a wide range of international and Polish artists, from rock and pop to electronic and alternative music. The festival takes place in a large park in the center of Warsaw.

- Wianki Świętojańskie: This traditional Polish midsummer festival celebrates the arrival of summer. The festival features bonfires, folk music and dance performances, and the crowning of a "Queen of the Meadow."

- Święto Niepodległości: This national holiday, celebrated on November 11th, commemorates Poland's regaining of independence in 1918. The holiday is marked by parades, concerts, and fireworks displays.

Additional Tips

- Check the official websites of the festivals and events for detailed information on dates, venues, and ticket prices.

- Book tickets in advance for popular events, especially during peak season.

- Consider purchasing a Warsaw Pass, which provides free or discounted admission to many museums, attractions, and cultural events.

- Explore the city's neighborhoods and discover hidden cultural gems, such as local theater productions, art exhibitions, and traditional music performances.

- Immerse yourself in the city's cultural scene by attending a variety of events, from traditional Polish celebrations to international arts and music festivals.

4.2 Art and Music Scene

Warsaw's art and music scene is a vibrant and dynamic reflection of the city's rich cultural heritage and contemporary spirit. From world-class museums and galleries to intimate concert venues and underground clubs, Warsaw offers a diverse range of artistic experiences for visitors to enjoy.

Museums and Galleries

Warsaw boasts a wealth of museums and galleries that showcase a wide spectrum of art, from classical masterpieces to contemporary works. Here are some of the must-visit museums and galleries for art enthusiasts:

- National Museum in Warsaw: This vast museum houses an extensive collection of Polish art, from medieval paintings to contemporary installations. The museum also features a collection of foreign art, including works by Rembrandt, Van Gogh, and Monet.

- Royal Castle Museum: This museum is located in the Royal Castle, a UNESCO World Heritage Site. The museum's collection includes royal portraits, furniture, and artifacts that provide insights into the lives of Polish monarchs.

- Museum of Modern Art in Warsaw: This museum showcases a collection of modern and contemporary art from Poland and around the world. The museum's collection includes works by Picasso, Kandinsky, and Polish artists such as Władysław Strzemiński and Tadeusz Kantor.

- Zachęta National Gallery of Art: This gallery hosts temporary exhibitions of contemporary art from Poland and abroad. The gallery also has a permanent collection of Polish art from the 20th and 21st centuries.

- Palace Gallery: This gallery is located in the Wilanów Palace, a Baroque masterpiece. The gallery hosts temporary exhibitions of art, design, and fashion.

Concert Venues and Clubs

Warsaw's music scene is as diverse as its art scene, with venues catering to a wide range of musical tastes. Here are some of the most popular concert venues and clubs in Warsaw:

- Polish National Opera: This opera house is one of the most prestigious in Europe. The opera house stages a variety of operas, ballets, and concerts.

- Warsaw Philharmonic Orchestra: This renowned orchestra performs a variety of classical music concerts throughout the year. The orchestra's home is the Warsaw Philharmonic Concert Hall, a beautiful concert hall located in the city center.

- National Forum of Music: This modern concert hall hosts a variety of musical performances, from classical to jazz to contemporary music. The venue also features a music museum and educational facilities.

- Stodoła: This historic club is one of the most popular live music venues in Warsaw. The club hosts a variety of concerts, from rock and pop to jazz and electronic music.

- Proxima: This intimate club is known for its eclectic programming, featuring local and international bands, DJs, and performers.

- Plan B: This underground club is a popular spot for alternative music, including punk, rock, and electronic music.

Additional Tips

- Check the listings in local newspapers and magazines for upcoming events and concerts.

- Follow the websites and social media pages of your favorite venues and artists to stay up-to-date on their events.

- Consider purchasing tickets in advance for popular events, especially during peak season.

- Explore the city's neighborhoods and discover hidden musical gems, such as local music bars, open mic nights, and street performances.

- Immerse yourself in Warsaw's vibrant music scene by attending a variety of concerts, from

4.3 Culinary Delights (Must-Try Dishes)

Embark on a culinary adventure through the heart of Warsaw and savor the authentic flavors of Polish cuisine. From hearty dumplings to comforting soups and savory stews, Polish cuisine offers a delightful symphony of tastes that will tantalize your palate. Discover the iconic dishes that are a must-try for any visitor to Warsaw.

1. Pierogi: These delectable dumplings, filled with a variety of savory or sweet fillings, are a staple of Polish cuisine. Indulge in the classic pierogi ruskie, filled with mashed potatoes, cheese, and onions, or explore other tempting varieties like pierogi with meat, sauerkraut, or sweet fruits.

2. Borscht: This hearty beet soup is a Polish culinary gem, warming the soul with its rich flavors and nourishing ingredients. Savor the classic borscht czerwony, a vibrant red beet soup, or try the refreshing chłodnik, a chilled beet soup perfect for summer days.

3. Żurek: This traditional sour rye soup is a unique and flavorful addition to your Polish culinary experience. Enjoy the hearty żurek with sausage, boiled eggs, and a touch of cream, or experiment with regional variations that incorporate mushrooms, potatoes, or white beans.

4. Bigos: This hunter's stew is a testament to Polish ingenuity, combining sauerkraut, meat, and various vegetables in a symphony of flavors. Immerse yourself in the rich aroma of bigos as it slowly simmers, and savor the comforting blend of flavors that this culinary masterpiece offers.

5. Kotlet Schabowy: This breaded pork cutlet is a beloved Polish comfort food, evoking a sense of nostalgia and home-cooked goodness. Enjoy the crispy, golden-brown cutlet served with traditional accompaniments like creamy mashed potatoes, fresh salads, and a touch of lingonberry jam.

Venture beyond these iconic dishes and explore the diverse culinary landscape of Warsaw. Indulge in regional specialties, discover hidden culinary gems tucked away in local neighborhoods, and immerse yourself in the vibrant food scene that reflects the city's rich cultural heritage.

4.4 Shopping in Warsaw

Warsaw offers a diverse range of shopping experiences, catering to every taste and budget. From traditional Polish handicrafts to international designer brands, you'll find a treasure trove of unique items to add to your collection.

Shopping Malls

Warsaw boasts several impressive shopping malls that offer a wide variety of stores, restaurants, and entertainment options. Here are some of the most popular shopping malls in Warsaw:

- Złote Tarasy: This sprawling mall is located in the city center and features over 200 stores, including international brands, local boutiques, and a variety of dining options.

- Arkadia: This modern mall is located in the northern part of Warsaw and offers over 230 stores, including international brands, Polish chains, and a multiplex cinema.

- Blue City: This vibrant mall is located in the western part of Warsaw and features over 200 stores, including international brands, local boutiques, and a grocery store.

- Galeria Mokotów: This upscale mall is located in the southern part of Warsaw and offers over 260 stores, including luxury brands, high-street retailers, and a variety of dining options.

- Madera: This outlet center is located on the outskirts of Warsaw and offers over 120 stores, including international brands, Polish chains, and a variety of dining options.

Shopping Streets

Warsaw also has several charming shopping streets lined with boutiques, cafes, and antique shops. Here are some of the most popular shopping streets in Warsaw:

- Nowy Świat: This elegant street is home to a variety of luxury brands, high-street retailers, and traditional Polish shops.

- Mokotowska: This trendy street is known for its designer boutiques, art galleries, and cafes.

- Marszałkowska: This bustling street is a mix of chain stores, local shops, and restaurants.

- Chmielna: This vibrant street is lined with cafes, bars, and boutiques.

- Bracka: This historic street is known for its antique shops, art galleries, and bookstores.

Markets

Warsaw has several lively markets where you can find fresh produce, handmade crafts, and souvenirs. Here are some of the most popular markets in Warsaw:

- Hala Mirowska: This historic market hall offers a wide variety of fresh produce, meat, fish, and dairy products.

- Hala Koszyki: This trendy market hall is home to a variety of restaurants, cafes, and shops selling food, flowers, and crafts.

- Targ Śniecki: This flea market is a treasure trove of antiques, collectibles, and vintage items.

- Sunday Market: This weekly market on Krakowskie Przedmieście street offers a variety of handmade crafts, souvenirs, and local food.

Tips for Shopping in Warsaw

- Bargaining is not common in Warsaw, but you may be able to negotiate a better price at flea markets and outdoor stalls.

- Many shops in Warsaw accept major credit cards, but it is always a good idea to have some cash on hand.

- The opening hours for shops vary, but most shops are open from 10:00 am to 8:00 pm, Monday to Saturday. On Sundays, certain stores are also open.

- Warsaw has a number of shopping malls that are open late, including Złote Tarasy, Arkadia, and Blue City.

- If you are looking for souvenirs, a good place to start is the Nowy Świat street, which is lined with shops selling traditional Polish handicrafts and souvenirs.

- For a more unique shopping experience, visit one of Warsaw's flea markets, such as Targ Śniecki or the Sunday Market on Krakowskie Przedmieście street.

CHAPTER 5: DAY TRIPS AND BEYOND

5.1 Excursions from Warsaw

Warsaw is a vibrant and exciting city, but there are also many fascinating places to visit within a short drive from the city center. Here are some suggestions for day trips from Warsaw:

1. Nieborów and Arkadia Palace: This picturesque town is located about 80 kilometers from Warsaw and is home to the beautiful Arkadia Palace, a masterpiece of 18th-century landscape architecture. The palace is surrounded by a park with numerous ponds, statues, and follies.

2. Kazimierz Dolny: This charming medieval town is located about 120 kilometers from Warsaw and is known for its Renaissance architecture, art galleries, and antique shops. Hiking and cycling are other popular activities in the town.

3. Łowicz: This historic town is located about 80 kilometers from Warsaw and is known for its colorful folk costumes and traditions. The town is home to the Regional Museum of Łowicz, which houses a collection of folk art and artifacts.

4. Puszcza Kampinoska National Park: This vast forest is located about 30 kilometers from Warsaw and is a UNESCO World Heritage Site. The park is home to a variety of wildlife, including wild boars, deer, and eagles. The park is a well-liked location for horseback riding, cycling, and hiking.

5. Żelazowa Wola: This small village is located about 60 kilometers from Warsaw and is the birthplace of Frédéric Chopin, Poland's renowned composer. The village is home to the Chopin Museum, which houses a collection of the composer's personal belongings and instruments.

Additional Tips

- Rent a car or hire a taxi for your day trip.

- Allow plenty of time for travel, especially if you are visiting a destination that is located further away from Warsaw.

- Check the opening hours of attractions before you go.

- Pack a picnic lunch or snacks for your trip.

- Bring sunscreen, sunglasses, and a hat if you are visiting during the summer months.

- Wear comfortable shoes for walking.

Enjoy your day trip from Warsaw!

5.2 Nearby Towns and Attractions

- Nieborów and Arkadia Palace: This picturesque town is located about 80 kilometers from Warsaw and is home to the beautiful Arkadia Palace, a masterpiece of 18th-century landscape architecture. The palace is surrounded by a park with numerous ponds, statues, and follies.

Nieborów and Arkadia Palace in Warsaw

- Kazimierz Dolny: This charming medieval town is located about 120 kilometers from Warsaw and is known for its Renaissance architecture, art galleries, and antique shops. The town is also a popular destination for hiking and cycling.

- Łowicz: This historic town is located about 80 kilometers from Warsaw and is known for its colorful folk costumes and traditions. The town is home to the Regional Museum of Łowicz, which houses a collection of folk art and artifacts.

- Puszcza Kampinoska National Park: This vast forest is located about 30 kilometers from Warsaw and is a UNESCO World Heritage Site. The park is home to a variety of wildlife, including wild boars, deer, and eagles. The park is a well-liked location for horseback riding, cycling, and hiking.

- Żelazowa Wola: This small village is located about 60 kilometers from Warsaw and is the birthplace of Frédéric Chopin, Poland's renowned composer. The village is home to the Chopin Museum, which houses a collection of the composer's personal belongings and instruments.

Other notable towns and attractions near Warsaw include:

- Częstochowa: A pilgrimage site with the Jasna Góra Monastery, home to the Black Madonna icon.

- Radom: A historic city with a medieval town center and a Renaissance cathedral.

- Kielce: A city known for its Świętokrzyskie Mountains, caves, and spas.

- Pułtusk: A charming town on the Vistula River with a Renaissance town square.

These are just a few of the many interesting towns and attractions that you can visit on a day trip from Warsaw. You're sure to find something to appreciate with so much to see and do.

5.3 Adventure Opportunities

Besides exploring nearby towns and historical landmarks, Warsaw offers a variety of adventure opportunities for those seeking an adrenaline rush or a unique outdoor experience. Here are some suggestions for adventurous activities near Warsaw:

1. Kayaking on the Vistula River: Paddle along the Vistula River, the heart of Warsaw, and immerse yourself in the city's captivating scenery from a different perspective. Enjoy the tranquil atmosphere and admire the iconic landmarks lining the riverbanks, such as the Royal Castle, the National Stadium, and the Copernicus Science Center.

2. Hiking in Kampinos National Park: Embark on a hiking adventure in Kampinos National Park, a vast wilderness just west of Warsaw. Explore the park's diverse landscapes, including lush forests, sandy plains, and picturesque lakes. Encounter a variety of wildlife, including deer, wild boars, and over 200 species of birds.

3. Cycling Through the Mazovia Region: Discover the beauty of the Mazovia region on a cycling tour. Choose from a variety of routes that wind through charming villages, picturesque countryside, and historical sites. Enjoy the fresh air, scenic views, and the opportunity to connect with nature.

4. Horseback Riding in the Kampinos Forest: Experience the thrill of horseback riding through the enchanting Kampinos Forest. Gallop through the verdant trails, surrounded by towering trees and the sounds of nature. Explore hidden paths and discover the forest's hidden gems.

5. Rock Climbing in Jura Krakowsko-Częstochowska: Challenge yourself with rock climbing in the Jura Krakowsko-Częstochowska region, known for its limestone cliffs and challenging climbing routes. Choose from various climbing grades, suitable for both beginners and experienced climbers.

6. Whitewater Rafting on the Dunajec River: Embark on an exhilarating whitewater rafting adventure on the Dunajec River, located south of Warsaw. Navigate the river's rapids and currents, surrounded by stunning mountain scenery. Experience the thrill of teamwork and the exhilaration of conquering the river's challenges.

7. Paragliding over the Mazovia Region: Take to the skies and enjoy a breathtaking paragliding experience over the Mazovia region. Soar above the rolling hills, verdant

forests, and picturesque lakes. Experience the freedom of flight and capture unforgettable aerial views of the countryside.

8. Paintball in the Kampinos Forest: Engage in a thrilling paintball battle in the heart of Kampinos Forest. Strategize with your team, navigate through obstacles, and test your shooting skills in a simulated combat environment. Experience the adrenaline rush and camaraderie of this competitive game.

9. Geocaching in the Warsaw Area: Embark on a geocaching adventure in the Warsaw area. Use a GPS device to find hidden caches, or geocaches, placed in various locations. Solve puzzles, decode clues, and explore hidden corners of the city while discovering new places and perspectives.

10. Escape Room Challenges in Warsaw: Challenge your mind and teamwork skills with an escape room experience in Warsaw. Solve puzzles, decipher clues, and work together to escape from a themed room within a set time limit. Experience the thrill of solving mysteries and the satisfaction of achieving the ultimate escape.

CHAPTER 6: ESSENTIAL TIPS FOR A MEMORABLE EXPERIENCE

6.1 Safety and Etiquette

To ensure a safe, enjoyable, and memorable trip to Warsaw, here are some essential tips to keep in mind:

Safety Tips

- Pay attention to your surroundings and stay away from carrying a lot of cash or valuables.
- Make sure your possessions are safe, especially in crowded places.
- Make use of ride-hailing services or authorized taxis.
- Don't go alone at night in dimly lit locations.
- Watch out for con artists and pickpockets.
- Follow your gut and stay away from uncomfortable circumstances.

Etiquette Tips

- Greetings: The common greeting in Poland is a handshake, accompanied by eye contact. For close friends or family, a hug or a kiss on both cheeks is also acceptable.

- Language: Poland's official language is Polish. While English is spoken in some tourist areas, learning a few basic Polish phrases will go a long way and show appreciation for the local culture.

- Dining Etiquette: When dining out, it's customary to wait for everyone at the table to be served before starting to eat. Tipping is not as common in Poland as in some other countries, but a small tip (5-10%) is appreciated for good service.

- Public Behavior: Be mindful of noise levels in public places, especially in churches, museums, and libraries. Smoking is prohibited in most public indoor spaces, including restaurants, bars, and public transportation.

- Dress Code: Dress appropriately for the occasion and the weather. While Warsaw is a cosmopolitan city, it's generally considered respectful to dress modestly when visiting religious sites or cultural institutions.

Additional Tips

- Learn about Polish history and culture to gain a deeper understanding of the country and its people.

- Plan your itinerary in advance to make the most of your time in Warsaw.

- Purchase a Warsaw Pass to save money on admission to museums and attractions.

- To guard against unanticipated incidents, think about getting travel insurance.

- Acquire some fundamental Polish language skills to improve your communication with locals.

- Be respectful of local customs and traditions.

- Enjoy the unique experiences and flavors that Warsaw has to offer.

6.2 Language Tips and Useful Phrases

Sure, here are some language tips and useful phrases for your trip to Warsaw:

Language Tips

- Polish pronunciation can be challenging for non-native speakers, but don't worry about making perfect mistakes. You'll get more respect from locals if you try to learn their language.

- Take note of these pronunciation guidelines:

    o The letter "ś" sounds like the "sh" in "shoe".

    o The letter "ż" sounds like the "zh" in "measure".

    o The letter "ą" sounds like the "om" in "comfort".

    o The letter "ę" sounds like the "an" in "canyon".

- Try to learn the Polish alphabet, as this will help you with pronunciation and recognizing signs and menus.

- Use a phrasebook or language learning app to learn basic Polish phrases.

Useful Phrases

Here are some useful Polish phrases to get you started:

- Greetings:
    - Dzień dobry (pronounced jen dobri) - Good day
    - Cześć (pronounced cheshch) - Hi
    - Dobry wieczór (pronounced dobri veechuhr) - Good evening
- Asking for directions:
    - Gdzie jest...? (pronounced gdje jest) - Where is...?
    - Jak dojadę do...? (pronounced yak doyado do) - How do I get to...?
    - Proszę pokazać mi na mapie (pronounced proszhe pokazach mi na mape) - Please show me on the map
- Basic conversation:
    - Tak (pronounced tak) - Yes
    - Nie (pronounced nie) - No
    - Proszę (pronounced proshe) - Please
    - Dziękuję (pronounced dzienkooye) - Thank you
    - Przepraszam (pronounced sheprafshawm) - Excuse me
    - Nie rozumiem (pronounced nie rozumiem) - I don't understand

- o Mówię po angielsku (pronounced mooviye po angyelsku) - I speak English

- Emergency phrases:
  - o Pomoc! (pronounced pomoch) - Help!
  - o Wzywam policję (pronounced veezhvam politse) - I call the police
  - o Potrzebuję lekarza (pronounced potrzebuje lekarza) - I need a doctor
  - o Jestem chory/chora (pronounced jestem chory/chora) - I am sick

These are only a few fundamental words to get you going. With a little effort, you'll be able to communicate effectively with locals and enhance your Warsaw experience.

6.3 Packing Suggestions

Packing for a trip to Warsaw, Poland should consider the city's climate, the time of year you're visiting, and your planned activities. Here's a comprehensive packing list for a Warsaw adventure:

1. Clothing:

a. Versatility: Pack versatile clothing items that can be mixed and matched to create different outfits. You'll be able to travel with less stuff and pack lighter as a result.

b. Layering: Layering is key for Warsaw's unpredictable weather. Bring a combination of lightweight T-shirts, long-sleeved shirts, sweaters, and a jacket to adapt to changing temperatures.

c. Footwear: Pack comfortable walking shoes as you'll be exploring the city on foot. Consider bringing an extra pair of shoes for wet weather or dressier occasions.

2. Accessories:

a. Scarf and Hat: Pack a scarf and hat to protect yourself from the cold and wind, especially during the winter months.

b. Sunglasses: Sunglasses are essential for protecting your eyes from the sun, especially during the summer months.

c. Rain Gear: Pack an umbrella or raincoat to be prepared for sudden showers.

3. Toiletries:

a. Essentials: Pack your essential toiletries, including shampoo, conditioner, soap, toothbrush, toothpaste, and any personal medications.

b. Sunscreen and Lotion: Bring sunscreen to protect your skin from the sun, especially during the summer months. Consider packing lotion to keep your skin hydrated, especially during the winter months.

4. Electronics:

a. Camera: Pack a camera to capture all the memories of your Warsaw trip. Consider bringing a portable charger to keep your camera battery powered up.

b. Phone and Charger: Don't forget your phone and charger to stay connected while in Warsaw.

c. Adapter: If you're traveling from outside of Europe, you'll need a travel adapter for your electronic devices.

5. Additional Items:

a. Day Bag: Pack a day bag to carry your essentials while exploring the city.

b. Guidebook or Phrasebook: A guidebook or phrasebook can be helpful for navigating the city and learning basic Polish phrases.

c. Currency Exchange: Exchange some currency for Polish zlotys (PLN) before your trip. You can also withdraw zlotys from ATMs in Warsaw.

6. Season-Specific Considerations:

a. Spring and Fall: Pack for a mix of warm and cool days. Bring a light jacket or coat for evenings and cooler weather.

b. Summer: Pack lightweight clothing, sunscreen, and a hat for sunny days. In case of unexpected rainfall, think about packing a raincoat or an umbrella.

c. Winter: Pack warm clothing, including a heavy coat, hat, gloves, and scarf. Be ready for chilly weather and snowfall.

Remember to check the weather forecast before you pack to get an idea of the temperatures you'll be facing. With careful planning and packing, you'll be well-prepared for an enjoyable and memorable Warsaw adventure.

ITINERARIES SUGGESTIONS

for a 3-day trip to Warsaw suggested itinerary

Day 1: Exploring the City Center

- Morning: Start your day at the Royal Castle, a symbol of Polish history and culture. Admire its Baroque architecture and explore its opulent interior, including the Royal Apartments, the Throne Room, and the Ballroom.

- Afternoon: Stroll through Castle Square, a vibrant plaza in the heart of Warsaw. Take in the lively atmosphere and admire the surrounding landmarks, such as Sigismund's Column and the Presidential Palace.

- Evening: Immerse yourself in Polish culture at the National Museum, home to a vast collection of art and artifacts from Poland and around the world. Explore its galleries and exhibitions to gain a deeper understanding of Polish history and heritage.

Day 2: Discovering Łazienki Park and the Warsaw Uprising Museum

- Morning: Escape the city's hustle and bustle in Łazienki Park, a serene oasis of greenery and tranquility. Stroll along its winding pathways, admire its picturesque landscapes, and relax by the tranquil lakes.

- Afternoon: Visit the Palace on the Water, a captivating Baroque palace situated on an island in the park. Explore its opulent interior, adorned with fine art, exquisite furnishings, and intricate tapestries.

- Evening: Pay your respects at the Warsaw Uprising Museum, a poignant reminder of the city's tumultuous past. Delve into the stories of courage and resilience during the 1944 uprising, and honor the sacrifices made for freedom.

Day 3: Venturing Beyond Warsaw

- Morning: Take a day trip to Wilanów Palace and Gardens, a UNESCO World Heritage Site located just outside Warsaw. Admire the palace's Baroque architecture and explore its lavishly decorated interior. Stroll through the sprawling gardens, a masterpiece of Baroque landscaping.

- Afternoon: Enjoy a leisurely lunch in Wilanów, savoring the flavors of Polish cuisine. Explore the charming streets and shops, and immerse yourself in the neighborhood's unique atmosphere.

- Evening: Return to Warsaw and conclude your trip with a traditional Polish dinner. Reflect on your experiences and bid farewell to this vibrant city, carrying with you the memories of its rich history and captivating culture.

7-day trip to Warsaw suggested itinerary:

Day 1: Exploring the City Center

- Morning: Start your day at the Royal Castle, a symbol of Polish history and culture. Admire its Baroque architecture and explore its opulent interior, including the Royal Apartments, the Throne Room, and the Ballroom.

- Afternoon: Stroll through Castle Square, a vibrant plaza in the heart of Warsaw. Take in the lively atmosphere and admire the surrounding landmarks, such as Sigismund's Column and the Presidential Palace.

- Evening: Immerse yourself in Polish culture at the National Museum, home to a vast collection of art and artifacts from Poland and around the world. Explore its galleries and exhibitions to gain a deeper understanding of Polish history and heritage.

Day 2: Discovering Łazienki Park and the Warsaw Uprising Museum

- Morning: Escape the city's hustle and bustle in Łazienki Park, a serene oasis of greenery and tranquility. Stroll along its winding pathways, admire its picturesque landscapes, and relax by the tranquil lakes.

- Afternoon: Visit the Palace on the Water, a captivating Baroque palace situated on an island in the park. Explore its opulent interior, adorned with fine art, exquisite furnishings, and intricate tapestries.

- Evening: Pay your respects at the Warsaw Uprising Museum, a poignant reminder of the city's tumultuous past. Delve into the stories of courage and resilience during the 1944 uprising, and honor the sacrifices made for freedom.

Day 3: Venturing Beyond Warsaw

- Morning: Take a day trip to Wilanów Palace and Gardens, a UNESCO World Heritage Site located just outside Warsaw. Admire the palace's Baroque architecture and explore its lavishly decorated interior. Stroll through the sprawling gardens, a masterpiece of Baroque landscaping.

- Afternoon: Enjoy a leisurely lunch in Wilanów, savoring the flavors of Polish cuisine. Explore the charming streets and shops, and immerse yourself in the neighborhood's unique atmosphere.

- Evening: Return to Warsaw and conclude your trip with a traditional Polish dinner. Reflect on your experiences and bid farewell to this vibrant city, carrying with you the memories of its rich history and captivating culture.

Day 4: Warsaw's Museums and Cultural Gems

- Morning: Visit the POLIN Museum of the History of Polish Jews, a captivating museum dedicated to the history and culture of Polish Jews. Explore its interactive exhibits and multimedia presentations to gain a deeper understanding of their rich heritage.

- Afternoon: Immerse yourself in the world of science at the Copernicus Science Center, a captivating museum designed to spark curiosity and inspire a love for science. Engage in hands-on experiments, explore interactive exhibits, and witness spectacular science shows.

- Evening: Enjoy a performance at the Polish National Opera, a renowned cultural institution with a rich history. Marvel at the exquisite opera house and immerse yourself in the world of music and theater.

Day 5: A Historical Journey

- Morning: Visit the Warsaw Ghetto Museum, a poignant reminder of the suffering and resilience of the Jewish people during World War II. Explore the museum's exhibits and multimedia presentations to gain a deeper understanding of the ghetto's tragic history.

- Afternoon: Pay your respects at the Museum of Freedom, dedicated to the struggle for Polish independence and the fight against totalitarianism. Explore the museum's exhibits and multimedia presentations to gain a deeper understanding of Poland's turbulent past.

- Evening: Stroll along the Royal Route, a historic walkway adorned with palaces, churches, and monuments. Experience the grandeur of Warsaw's past and admire the city's architectural heritage.

Day 6: Warsaw's Green Spaces and Recreational Activities

- Morning: Escape the city's hustle and bustle in Siemienski Park, a picturesque park with lush greenery, walking paths, and a charming restaurant. Take a leisurely stroll, enjoy a picnic lunch, or rent a bike to explore the park's trails.

- Afternoon: Embark on a scenic Vistula River cruise, offering panoramic views of Warsaw's iconic landmarks from a different perspective. Relax on the deck, enjoy the breeze, and capture memorable photos of the city skyline.

- Evening: Visit the Warsaw Zoo, home to a diverse range of animals from around the world. Observe the animals in their natural habitats, learn about conservation efforts, and enjoy a unique wildlife experience.

Day 7: Experiencing Warsaw's Culinary Delights

- Morning: Indulge in a traditional Polish breakfast at a local cafe, savoring favorites like pierogi (dumplings), zapiekanka (open-faced sandwiches), and oscypek (smoked cheese).

- Afternoon: Embark on a food tour of Warsaw, exploring hidden gems and indulging in authentic Polish cuisine. Sample local delicacies, discover traditional recipes, and gain insights into Polish food culture.

- Evening: Enjoy a farewell dinner at a renowned Polish restaurant, savoring

CONCLUSION

As you say goodbye to Warsaw, its colorful soul will live on in your mind, a symphony of sights, sounds, and tastes that have infused your travels with enchanting colors. You've explored the halls of history, descended into the depths of culture, and indulged in delectable cuisine, turning an ordinary trip into an incredible journey.

This guide has been your constant companion, your translator of local folklore, your passport to undiscovered treasures, and your route through the maze-like alleys. Always keep in mind that Warsaw is more than just a place to visit; it's a dynamic mosaic of history, culture, and passion. Its beauty also gradually becomes apparent with each viewing, much like that of any exquisite tapestry.

Leave Warsaw with a grin on your face, for it has given you lifelong memories to remember. Traveler, go forth and carry the spirit of Warsaw with you, enchanting the world with your enthralling tales and contagious pleasure.

I am grateful that you have joined me on this literary adventure. It is my goal that my words have given you a clear picture of Warsaw and encouraged you to discover all of its features. I hope the spirit of surprise and discovery you've felt in this enchanted city continues to accompany you on your future journeys.

Keep smiling and have a happy journey until we cross paths again in the pages of another adventure!

Printed in Great Britain
by Amazon

40959045R00046